TREES

A Compare and Contrast Book
By Katharine Hall

Trees are plants with a woody stem, called a trunk.

Trees can plant their roots in water . . .

. . . on rocks . . .

. . . or in soil. The soil near this tree has eroded so that the roots are exposed.

This oak tree lives
in a forest with
many other trees.

But this acacia tree thrives alone.

Trees can live in warm climates,
like this Joshua tree.

And trees can live in cold climates, like these black spruce pines.

Some trees, like this satsuki azalea bonsai, are very small even when fully grown. Other trees are very tall. The giant redwood is the tallest tree in the world.

Deciduous trees shed their leaves once a year. The leaves on many deciduous trees change color before falling from the tree.

Evergreen trees keep their leaves
and stay green all year round.

Trees with wide, flat leaves are called broadleaf trees. Other trees have scaly, needlelike leaves and are called conifers.

Many different kinds of trees grow all around the world, on every continent except Antarctica.

For Creative Minds

Trees Help Me Breathe!

Humans rely on trees and other plants for the air we need to live! Air is made of a mixture of different gases. Most of the air is nitrogen, oxygen and carbon dioxide. When humans breathe in air, we absorb oxygen into our lungs and then exhale carbon dioxide.

Unlike animals that must eat to get energy, plants make their own energy through a process called photosynthesis. To complete photosynthesis, plants need carbon dioxide, water, and sunlight. Plants take in carbon dioxide from the air and water from the ground, through their roots. Chlorophyll in the leaves absorbs energy from the sunlight. Plants use the sun's energy to create a sugary food made from water and carbon dioxide. After absorbing carbon dioxide, plants create oxygen and release it into the air for humans and other animals to breathe.

One adult tree can absorb as much as 48 pounds (21.7 kg) of carbon dioxide each year. Some trees can also help filter out pollution from the air. Trees in large cities have to be highly resistant to air pollution. Other trees cannot survive in heavily polluted areas.

What Else do Trees do for Me?

Living trees are necessary for humans to live and breathe. But after a tree dies, it becomes a natural resource that can be used by humans in many different ways! Look at the items below and see if you can tell which are made using parts of old trees.

cork

book

violin

chair

railroad crossties

pencils

picnic tables

notebook

playground woodchips

Answer: All of them!

Tree Parts

Trees have many different parts that allow the plant to grow, live, and reproduce. Match the description to the image.

 A.

 B.

 C.

 D.

1. Like all living things, trees must reproduce. Trees grow **flowers** that create pollen. Pollen is carried from one flower to another by wind, water, and insects. After the flower has been pollinated, it produces a seed. Many tree seeds grow inside fruits, nuts, or cones. A seed can be planted and grow into a whole new tree.

2. Trees absorb energy from sunlight through their **leaves**. Flat and wide leaves take in more energy from the sun. Small and scaly leaves are better at surviving harsh weather conditions.

3. The **trunk** supports the weight of the tree and holds the branches, flowers, and leaves up off the ground. Many animals find or build their homes in trees. Some animals find or burrow holes in the trunk to make a nest inside the tree. Other animals build nests supported by the tree's branches.

4. Trees absorb water and nutrients through their **roots**. The roots are usually below the ground and anchor the plant in place so it doesn't fall over or blow away. Some trees have roots that extend deep into the soil. Other trees have shallow root systems that branch out to all sides just at or under the surface.

Answers: 1-A, 2-C, 3-D, 4-B

Trees and Animals

Trees are an important part of the habitat for many kinds of animals. Many animals, including humans, eat food that comes from trees. Some animals eat bark or leaves. Others eat the fruits and nuts that trees produce.

Trees provide shade that keeps an area cool. Humans and other animals often rest under a tree to escape from the hot sun. In the heat of summer, shade from trees can mean a difference of 20°F (11°C)!

Many animals build their homes in and around trees. Spiders spin their webs from tree to tree. Rodents like gophers and mice dig holes near the tree's roots. This bird, a weaver finch, is building a nest in the branches of a tree.

Predators like this jaguar can wait in a tree for their prey and then pounce on them from above!

Prey animals like this squirrel can scurry up into a tree to escape from a predator on the ground.

To my sisters, Rachel and Helen, and all the friends who have climbed trees with me through the years.—KH

Thanks to Jaclyn Stallard, Manager of Education Programs at Project Learning Tree (www.plt.org) for verifying the accuracy of the information in this book.

Library of Congress Cataloging-in-Publication Data

Hall, Katharine, 1989-
  Trees : a compare and contrast book / by Katharine Hall.
    pages cm. -- (Compare and contrast books)
  ISBN 978-1-62855-453-3 (english hardcover) -- ISBN 978-1-62855-461-8 (english pbk.) -- ISBN 978-1-62855-477-9 (english downloadable ebook) -- ISBN 978-1-62855-493-9 (english interactive dual-language ebook) -- ISBN 978-1-62855-469-4 (spanish pbk.) -- ISBN 978-1-62855-485-4 (spanish downloadable ebook) -- ISBN 978-1-62855-501-1 (spanish interactive dual-language ebook) 1. Trees--Juvenile literature. I. Title.
  QK475.8.H35 2014
  582.16--dc23
                  2014011129

Translated into Spanish: Árboles: un libro de comparación y contraste   Lexile® Level: 690
key phrases for educators: antonyms/synonyms, compare/contrast, EE (Environmental Education), habitat, plants, weather/climate

Bibliography:

Kuhns, Michael. "What is a Tree?." Utah State University. Accessed December 2013. <http://forestry.usu.edu/htm/treeid/what-is-a-tree-youth>.

"Trees and Vegetation." United States Environmental Protection Agency. Accessed January 2014. <http://www.epa.gov/heatisland/mitigation/trees.htm>.

Thanks to Terry Hall for the use of his photographs for this book, to Andrew F. Kazmierski for allowing the purchase of his photograph through shutterstock, and to the remaining photographers and organizations for releasing their images into the public domain.

Photo	Photographer or Organization
Cover	Terry Hall
Title Page	Terry Hall
September in the Forest	Larisa Koshkina
Mangrove	Steve Hillebrand, USFWS
Rocks and Roots	Lilla Frerichs
Tree Roots	Larisa Koshkina
Forest, Spanish Moss	Steve Hillebrand, USFWS
Umbrella Thorn Acacia Tree	Gary M. Stolz, USFWS
Joshua tree & stone landscape	Andrew F. Kazmierski , Shutterstock
Denali trees in winter	Tim Rains, National Park Service
Bonsai	Michael Drummond
Redwood	National Park Service
Autumn Landscape	Larisa Koshkina
Evergreens in Winter	Terry Hall
Maple Leaves	Ryan Hagerty, USFWS
Conifer and Snow	Terry Hall
Forest background	George Gentry, USFWS
Skyline and City Streets	Alex Grichenko
Book	George Hodan
Wooden Chair	Petr Kratochvil
Cork	Kajoch Adras
Spiral Notepad	Karen Arnold
Colored Pencils	Petr Kratochvil
Picnic table	Darren Lewis
Playground	Peter Griffin
Tracks to nowhere	Scott Meltzer
Violin	Katrina Joyner
Flowering Tree	Jeanette ONeil
Various Fruits	Petr Kratochvil
Nuts	Petr Kratochvil
Jaguar on Tree Trunk	Lilla Frerichs
Squirrel	George Hodan
Picnic Table Under Tree	Lilla Frerichs
Weaver Bird Weaving Nest	Lilla Frerichs

Manufactured in China, November 2014
This product conforms to CPSIA 2008
First Printing

Arbordale Publishing
Mt. Pleasant, SC 29464
www.ArbordalePublishing.com